Spiritual 911- God's Word for Life's Emergency's

Joshua Rhoades

Published by Joshua Paul Rhoades, 2024.

SPIRITUAL 911- GOD'S WORD FOR LIFE'S EMERGENCY'S

First edition. August 31, 2024.

ISBN: 979-8227134882

Written by Joshua Rhoades.

Also by Joshua Rhoades

Courage Under Fire: David's Stand On The Battlefield
Jonah's Journey: Voices Of Redemption And Lessons In Obedience
The Furnace Of Faith: 12 Principles From The Heat Of Faith
Whispers of Hope: Inspiring Stories of Men's Prayers In Scripture
Frontier Legends: The Oregon Dream
Elijah: A Beacon Of Boldness
HOOK, LINE & SAVIOUR - Faith Reflections from Fishing
Driven By Faith: Motor Racing Inspired Christian Life
30 Day Devotional - Bold and Strong- Coffee Devotions for a
Courageous Christian Walk
Authentic Christianity: The Heart of Old Time Religion
Consider The Ant - God's Tiny Preachers
Flee Fornication: The Plea For Purity
Renewed Hope- How to Find Encouragement in God
Sounding The Call - The Voice of Conviction
The Altar - Where Heaven Meets Earth
The Bible's Battlefields- Timeless Lessons from Ancient Wars
The Sacred Art of Silence - How Silence Speaks in Scripture
Under Fire- The Sanctity of the Traditional Biblical Home
Who Is on the Lord's Side? A Call to Righteousness
What Is Truth? - From Skepticism to Submission
First and Goal- Faith and Football Fundamentals
From Dugout to Devotion- Spiritual Lessons from Baseball
Par for the Course- Faith and Fairways
The Believer's Pace- Tools for Running Life's Marathon

The Immutable Fortress- Security in God's Unchanging Nature
Biblical Bravery
Deer Stands and Devotions: A Hunter's Walk with God
Jesus Knows- Our Hearts, Our Responsibility
Restoration - Setting The Bone
Spiritual 911- God's Word for Life's Emergency's
The Freedom of Forgiveness
The Jezebel Effect - Ancient Manipulations Modern Lessons
The Shout That Stopped The Saviour

Introduction

Chapter 1 -If You Are Feeling Depressed – Psalms 27

Chapter 2 – When You Are Lonely – Psalms 23

Chapter 3 – When You Want Courage – Joshua 1

Chapter 4 – If People Seem Unkind – John 15

Chapter 5 – When Your Faith Needs. Stirring – Hebrews 11

Chapter 6 – When You Have Sinned – Psalms 51

Chapter 7 – When You Worry – Matthew 6:19-34

Chapter 8 – When God Seems Far Away – Psalms 139

Chapter 9 – When You Are Bitter – I Corinthians 13

Chapter 10 – When You Are In Danger – Psalms 91

Chapter 11 – If Your Wallet Is Empty – Psalms 37

Chapter 12 – Christian Assurance – Romans 8:1-30

Chapter 13 – When Your Prayers Grow Selfish – Psalms 67

Chapter 14 – For A Great Opportunity – Isaiah 55

Chapter 15 – When You Leave To Travel – Psalms 123

Conclusion

Introduction

When faced with an emergency, our first instinct is to dial 911. We know that in moments of crisis, help is just a call away, and the assurance of professional assistance brings us comfort and security. In the same way, as Christians, we have a spiritual emergency line available to us through the Word of God. The Bible is our divine 911, filled with chapters that provide learning, conviction, and comfort. This book is designed to be your spiritual guide, directing you to specific scriptures that you can "call" upon in various life situations. Just as we trust emergency services to respond in our time of need, we can trust God's Word to provide the guidance and solace we need.

Every chapter of this book is a call to delve deeper into the scriptures, discovering the blessings that come from turning to God in times of joy, sorrow, uncertainty, and gratitude. For example, when you are overwhelmed with worry, you can "call" on Matthew 6:19-34 to find reassurance in God's provision and care. When facing a great opportunity, Isaiah 55 can remind you of God's call to seek Him and trust in His higher ways. Each chapter is a reminder that God's Word is living and active, a source of strength and direction for every situation.

As you journey through this book, you will learn to rely on the Bible as your ultimate emergency resource. By reflecting on these scriptures, you can gain wisdom for decision-making, find comfort in times of distress, and experience the transformative power of God's promises. The practical insights shared in each chapter are meant to help you apply these biblical truths to your daily life, enhancing your spiritual growth and strengthening your faith.

After reading this book, you are encouraged to proceed with a heart open to the leading of the Holy Spirit. Make it a habit to turn to the Bible first in every circumstance. Let the scriptures become a natural response to life's challenges and joys. Keep a journal to record the insights and revelations you receive, and share these blessings with others. Encourage your family, friends, and fellow believers to also rely on the Bible as their spiritual 911, creating a community grounded in God's Word.

This book is not just a guide but an invitation to experience the richness of a life connected to the scriptures. May it inspire you to call on the Lord in every situation, trusting that He will answer and provide exactly what you need. Embrace the blessings of learning, conviction, and comfort that come from God's Word, and let it transform your life from one of spiritual emergency to one of divine assurance and peace.

Chapter 1 -If You Are Feeling Depressed – Psalms 27

If you are feeling depressed, the Bible can be a great source of comfort and hope. One particular chapter that many people turn to in times of trouble is Psalm 27 from the King James Version. This psalm, written by King David, expresses trust in the Lord's protection and guidance even in the face of fear and adversity. The opening verse, Psalm 27:1, states, "The Lord is my light and my salvation; whom shall I fear? the Lord is the strength of my life; of whom shall I be afraid?" This verse reminds us that the Lord is always with us, providing light and strength in the darkest times, so we need not be afraid. As you read further, Psalm 27:3 offers reassurance: "Though an host should encamp against me, my heart shall not fear: though war should rise against me, in this will I be confident." This teaches us that even when we are surrounded by troubles and conflicts, we can remain confident because of our faith in God. Continuing, Psalm 27:4 highlights the importance of seeking God's presence: "One thing have I desired of the Lord, that will I seek after; that I may dwell in the house of the Lord all the days of my life, to behold the beauty of the Lord, and to enquire in his temple." This verse encourages us to focus on our relationship with God, finding solace in His presence and the beauty of His creation. In times of depression, it can be comforting to remember that we are always welcome in God's house and can seek His guidance and love.

In Psalm 27:5, David expresses his faith in God's protection: "For in the time of trouble he shall hide me in his pavilion: in the secret of his tabernacle shall he hide me; he shall set me up upon a rock." This verse assures us that God provides a safe place for us during difficult times, shielding us from harm and lifting us up above our troubles. It's a reminder that we are never alone and that God is always there to protect and support us. Further on, Psalm 27:7-8 shows David calling out to

God and seeking His face: "Hear, O Lord, when I cry with my voice: have mercy also upon me, and answer me. When thou saidst, Seek ye my face; my heart said unto thee, Thy face, Lord, will I seek." These verses emphasize the importance of reaching out to God in prayer and seeking His presence. When we feel overwhelmed or depressed, turning to God in prayer can provide comfort and guidance.

Psalm 27:10 offers hope and reassurance even when we feel abandoned: "When my father and my mother forsake me, then the Lord will take me up." This verse tells us that even if we feel forsaken by those closest to us, God will never abandon us. He will always be there to lift us up and care for us, providing a sense of belonging and security.

In Psalm 27:13-14, David concludes with a message of hope and patience: "I had fainted, unless I had believed to see the goodness of the Lord in the land of the living. Wait on the Lord: be of good courage, and he shall strengthen thine heart: wait, I say, on the Lord." These verses remind us that even when we feel like giving up, believing in God's goodness and waiting on His timing can give us the strength to endure. Patience and faith are crucial when dealing with depression, as they help us trust that God has a plan and will bring us through our struggles.

Turning to the Bible and reading Psalm 27 can provide comfort and strength during times of depression. The verses remind us of God's constant presence, protection, and love, encouraging us to seek Him, trust in His plan, and find peace in His promises. By applying the lessons of Psalm 27 to our lives, we can find hope and resilience in the face of our darkest moments, knowing that God is always with us and will never forsake us.

Chapter 2 – When You Are Lonely – Psalms 23

One of the most comforting passages is Psalm 23. Psalm 23, written by King David, is a beautiful reminder of God's constant presence and care in our lives. It begins with the well-known words, "The Lord is my shepherd; I shall not want." This means that God is like a shepherd who takes care of his sheep, providing for all our needs. When we feel lonely, it is comforting to remember that God is always watching over us and making sure we have what we need.

The next verse, Psalm 23:2, says, "He maketh me to lie down in green pastures: he leadeth me beside the still waters." This imagery of green pastures and still waters is very peaceful and reassuring. It reminds us that God leads us to places of rest and peace, even when we feel alone and troubled. He gives us a sense of calm and security that can help us through our lonely times. Psalm 23:3 continues, "He restoreth my soul: he leadeth me in the paths of righteousness for his name's sake." Here, we are reminded that God restores our souls, giving us strength and guiding us on the right path. When we feel lonely, it can be hard to find direction or purpose, but this verse reassures us that God is guiding us every step of the way and helping us to live rightly.

One of the most powerful verses in this psalm is Psalm 23:4: "Yea, though I walk through the valley of the shadow of death, I will fear no evil: for thou art with me; thy rod and thy staff they comfort me." This verse tells us that even in the darkest and most frightening times, we do not need to be afraid because God is with us. His rod and staff, tools a shepherd uses to protect and guide his sheep, symbolize God's protection and guidance. Knowing that God is with us, even in the hardest times, can bring great comfort when we feel lonely and scared.

Psalm 23:5 offers a beautiful image of God's care and provision: "Thou preparest a table before me in the presence of mine enemies: thou anointest my head with oil; my cup runneth over." This verse shows that God not only protects us but also blesses us abundantly, even in the face of difficulties. The image of a table prepared for us and a cup that overflows signifies God's generous blessings and care. When we feel lonely, remembering that God is actively providing for us can help us feel less alone and more secure in His love.

The final verse, Psalm 23:6, wraps up this comforting message with hope and assurance: "Surely goodness and mercy shall follow me all the days of my life: and I will dwell in the house of the Lord for ever." This verse promises that God's goodness and mercy will be with us throughout our lives and that we will have a place with Him forever. This eternal perspective can help us feel less lonely, knowing that we have an everlasting relationship with God and a home with Him.

Turning to Psalm 23 when we feel lonely can remind us of God's constant presence, protection, and provision. The verses of this psalm paint a picture of a loving and caring shepherd who looks after his sheep, ensuring they have everything they need and are safe from harm. This imagery can bring peace and comfort, helping us to remember that we are never truly alone. God's love and care are with us always, guiding us through life's challenges and leading us to places of rest and peace.

When loneliness creeps in, reading and reflecting on Psalm 23 can help shift our focus from our feelings of isolation to the reality of God's unwavering companionship. By meditating on these verses, we can find reassurance in God's promises and feel a sense of peace and comfort that transcends our current circumstances. This psalm encourages us to trust in God's guidance and to find solace in His presence, no matter what we are going through.

Furthermore, applying the truths of Psalm 23 to our daily lives can help us build a deeper relationship with God. By regularly spending time in prayer and reflection, we can become more aware of His presence and more attuned to His guidance. This practice can help us feel more connected to God and less overwhelmed by feelings of loneliness.

Additionally, reaching out to others and sharing the comfort we find in Psalm 23 can help build supportive relationships and create a sense of community.

In conclusion, Psalm 23 is a powerful passage to turn to when we feel lonely. Its verses remind us that God is our shepherd, always watching over us, providing for our needs, and guiding us through life's challenges. By meditating on this psalm, we can find comfort and reassurance in God's constant presence and love. This knowledge can help us feel less alone and more secure in our relationship with Him. By applying the truths of Psalm 23 to our lives and sharing its message with others, we can build a stronger connection with God and create a supportive community that helps alleviate feelings of loneliness.

Chapter 3 – When You Want Courage – Joshua 1

When you need courage, the Bible offers many verses that can inspire and strengthen you, and one of the best places to turn is Joshua 1. This chapter is filled with words of encouragement and guidance from God to Joshua as he prepares to lead the Israelites into the Promised Land. It begins with God speaking to Joshua after the death of Moses, saying, "Moses my servant is dead; now therefore arise, go over this Jordan, thou, and all this people, unto the land which I do give to them, even to the children of Israel." (Joshua 1:2). Here, God is calling Joshua to step up and take on the responsibility of leading the people, reminding him that the land is a gift from God.

In Joshua 1:3, God promises Joshua, "Every place that the sole of your foot shall tread upon, that have I given unto you, as I said unto Moses." This verse reassures Joshua that God's promises are still in effect and that He will fulfill them. When we seek courage, it is comforting to know that God keeps His promises and that we can trust in His word. God further assures Joshua in verse 5: "There shall not any man be able to stand before thee all the days of thy life: as I was with Moses, so I will be with thee: I will not fail thee, nor forsake thee." This powerful promise reminds us that God is always with us, just as He was with Moses, and that He will never abandon us. Knowing that God is on our side can give us the courage to face any challenge.

One of the key verses in this chapter is Joshua 1:6, where God commands Joshua, "Be strong and of a good courage: for unto this people shalt thou divide for an inheritance the land, which I sware unto their fathers to give them." Here, God is telling Joshua to be strong and courageous because he has an important task ahead of him. This verse reminds us that courage is essential when we have responsibilities and goals to achieve. We are encouraged to be strong and brave, knowing that God has a purpose for us and will help us accomplish it.

God continues to encourage Joshua in verse 7, saying, "Only be thou strong and very courageous, that thou mayest observe to do according to all the law, which Moses my servant commanded thee: turn not from it to the right hand or to the left, that thou mayest prosper whithersoever thou goest." This verse highlights the importance of following God's commandments and staying true to His word. By doing so, we can find the strength and courage to succeed in whatever we do. It is a reminder that obedience to God's laws and principles is key to living a courageous and prosperous life.

In Joshua 1:8, God provides further instruction: "This book of the law shall not depart out of thy mouth; but thou shalt meditate therein day and night, that thou mayest observe to do according to all that is written therein: for then thou shalt make thy way prosperous, and then thou shalt have good success." This verse emphasizes the importance of studying and meditating on God's word regularly. When we immerse ourselves in the Bible and live according to its teachings, we gain wisdom, guidance, and the courage to face life's challenges. By keeping God's word in our hearts and minds, we can navigate our paths with confidence and faith.

God's command to be strong and courageous is repeated again in Joshua 1:9, where He says, "Have not I commanded thee? Be strong and of a good courage; be not afraid, neither be thou dismayed: for the Lord thy God is with thee whithersoever thou goest." This powerful verse reassures us that we should not be afraid or discouraged because God is always with us. His presence provides us with the strength and courage we need to overcome any obstacle. When we feel fear or doubt, we can draw on this promise and find the confidence to move forward, knowing that God is by our side.

The rest of the chapter describes how Joshua prepares the people for their journey into the Promised Land. In verses 10 and 11, Joshua commands the officers of the people, saying, "Pass through the host, and command the people, saying, Prepare you victuals; for within three days ye shall pass over this Jordan, to go in to possess the land, which the Lord your God giveth you to possess it." This shows Joshua's leadership and the importance of preparation and readiness. By following God's guidance and preparing themselves, the Israelites demonstrate their trust in God's promise and their willingness to take action.

In verses 16-18, the people respond to Joshua's commands with loyalty and commitment, saying, "All that thou commandest us we will do, and whithersoever thou sendest us, we will go. According as we hearkened unto Moses in all things, so will we hearken unto thee: only the Lord thy God be with thee, as he was with Moses. Whosoever he be that doth rebel against thy commandment, and will not hearken unto thy words in all that thou commandest him, he shall be put to death: only be strong and of a good courage." The people's response underscores the importance of unity, obedience, and mutual support in achieving their goals. Their commitment to following Joshua's leadership, combined with their faith in God's presence, helps to strengthen their resolve and courage.

Joshua 1 provides a powerful message about the importance of courage, faith, and obedience to God's word. By reflecting on the promises and commands given to Joshua, we can find the strength and courage to face our own challenges. God's assurances that He will always be with us, that He will not fail or forsake us, and that He will help us prosper and succeed are timeless truths that can inspire and empower us in our daily lives.

When we are in need of courage, turning to Joshua 1 can remind us of God's unwavering support and guidance. The chapter encourages us to be strong and courageous, to trust in God's promises, and to follow His commandments. By doing so, we can find the confidence and resilience to overcome obstacles and achieve our goals. Additionally, immersing ourselves in God's word and meditating on His teachings can provide the wisdom and direction we need to navigate life's challenges with faith and determination.

Moreover, the example of Joshua's leadership and the people's response highlights the importance of preparation, readiness, and unity. When we work together, support one another, and stay true to our commitments, we can accomplish great things. This chapter also teaches us the value of trusting in God's plan and taking action with confidence, knowing that He is with us every step of the way.

In conclusion, Joshua 1 is a powerful source of inspiration and encouragement when we need courage. The chapter's messages of strength, faith, and obedience to God's word provide a solid foundation for overcoming fear and doubt. By reflecting on these verses and applying their lessons to our lives, we can find the courage to face any challenge and achieve our goals with confidence. Trusting in God's promises and presence, following His guidance, and supporting one another can help us navigate life's difficulties with resilience and hope. Through the timeless truths found in Joshua 1, we can draw strength and courage from our faith, knowing that God is always with us and will never forsake us.

Chapter 4 – If People Seem Unkind – John 15

The Bible has some great advice and comfort for these times, especially in John 15. In this chapter, Jesus talks to His disciples and gives them important teachings about love, friendship, and staying strong in faith. These teachings can help us understand how to deal with unkindness and find strength and comfort in God's love.

John 15 begins with Jesus saying, "I am the true vine, and my Father is the husbandman. Every branch in me that beareth not fruit he taketh away: and every branch that beareth fruit, he purgeth it, that it may bring forth more fruit." (John 15:1-2). Jesus is explaining that He is like a vine and we are the branches. God the Father is the gardener who takes care of the vine. If we stay connected to Jesus, like branches to a vine, we can grow and produce good fruit, which means good deeds and love. When people are unkind, remembering that we are connected to Jesus can help us stay strong and not be influenced by their negativity. In John 15:4, Jesus says, "Abide in me, and I in you. As the branch cannot bear fruit of itself, except it abide in the vine; no more can ye, except ye abide in me." This means that we need to stay close to Jesus and keep our faith in Him. Just like a branch needs the vine to grow, we need Jesus to help us be kind and loving, even when others are not. By staying connected to Him through prayer, reading the Bible, and following His teachings, we can find the strength to deal with unkindness.

Jesus continues in John 15:5, saying, "I am the vine, ye are the branches: He that abideth in me, and I in him, the same bringeth forth much fruit: for without me ye can do nothing." This verse reminds us that we can do good things and show love only with Jesus' help. When people are unkind, it's easy to get angry or upset, but if we remember to stay close to Jesus, we can respond with kindness and patience instead.

In John 15:9, Jesus says, "As the Father hath loved me, so have I loved you: continue ye in my love." This verse is a powerful reminder of how much Jesus loves us. Just as God the Father loves Jesus, Jesus loves us with that same perfect love. When people are unkind, we can find comfort in knowing that Jesus loves us deeply and unconditionally. His love can give us the strength to face unkindness and respond with love and compassion.

One of the most important teachings in John 15 is found in verse 12: "This is my commandment, That ye love one another, as I have loved you." Jesus commands us to love each other just as He loves us. This means showing kindness, understanding, and forgiveness, even when others are not kind to us. Loving others, especially when it's difficult, is a powerful way to show our faith and follow Jesus' example.

In John 15:13, Jesus explains what true love is: "Greater love hath no man than this, that a man lay down his life for his friends." Jesus showed the greatest love by giving His life for us. This verse encourages us to be willing to make sacrifices and put others' needs before our own. When we face unkindness, remembering Jesus' ultimate act of love can inspire us to be kind and loving in return.

Jesus also talks about friendship in John 15:14-15, saying, "Ye are my friends, if ye do whatsoever I command you. Henceforth I call you not servants; for the servant knoweth not what his lord doeth: but I have called you friends; for all things that I have heard of my Father I have made known unto you." Jesus calls us His friends if we follow His commandments. This special relationship with Jesus can give us comfort and strength when we face unkindness. Knowing that Jesus sees us as His friends means we are never alone, even when others are unkind.

Another important verse is John 15:16, where Jesus says, "Ye have not chosen me, but I have chosen you, and ordained you, that ye should go and bring forth fruit, and that your fruit should remain: that whatsoever ye shall ask of the Father in my name, he may give it you." Jesus chose us and wants us to live a life that bears good fruit, which means showing love and kindness to others. When people are unkind, we can remember that Jesus has a purpose for us, and He will help us grow and remain strong in our faith.

In John 15:18-19, Jesus warns His disciples about facing unkindness and hatred: "If the world hate you, ye know that it hated me before it hated you. If ye were of the world, the world would love his own: but because ye are not of the world, but I have chosen you out of the world, therefore the world hateth you." These verses remind us that being a follower of Jesus might mean facing unkindness from others. But we can take comfort in knowing that Jesus faced the same things and understands what we are going through. His words encourage us to stay strong and not be discouraged when people are unkind because we are chosen and loved by Him. Jesus continues to offer comfort in John 15:20, saying, "Remember the word that I said unto you, The servant is not greater than his lord. If they have persecuted me, they will also persecute you; if they have kept my saying, they will keep yours also." This verse reminds us that we should expect to face challenges and unkindness just as Jesus did. But it also reassures us that some people will listen and respond positively to our kindness and faith. By remembering Jesus' teachings and staying strong in our faith, we can navigate through times of unkindness with grace.

In John 15:26-27, Jesus talks about the Comforter, the Holy Spirit: "But when the Comforter is come, whom I will send unto you from the Father, even the Spirit of truth, which proceedeth from the Father, he shall testify of me: And ye also shall bear witness, because ye have been with me from the beginning." Jesus promises to send the Holy Spirit to guide, comfort, and strengthen us. When we face unkindness, we can rely on the Holy Spirit to help us respond with love and patience. The Holy Spirit also helps us to be witnesses of Jesus' love and truth, even in difficult situations.

Turning to John 15 when we face unkindness can remind us of the love, friendship, and support we have in Jesus. The chapter encourages us to stay connected to Jesus, to love others as He loves us, and to find comfort in His presence and the guidance of the Holy Spirit. By following these teachings, we can respond to unkindness with kindness, patience, and grace.

Moreover, applying the lessons from John 15 to our lives can help us build stronger, more loving relationships. By staying close to Jesus through prayer, reading the Bible, and living according to His teachings, we can find the strength and courage to face unkindness. We can also be inspired to show love and kindness to others, even when it is difficult, and to be a positive example of Jesus' love in the world.

In conclusion, John 15 is a powerful source of comfort and guidance when we face unkindness. The teachings of Jesus in this chapter remind us of His love, the importance of staying connected to Him, and the power of the Holy Spirit to guide and comfort us. By reflecting on these verses and applying their lessons to our lives, we can find the strength and courage to respond to unkindness with love and patience. Trusting in Jesus' promises and staying strong in our faith can help us navigate through difficult times and build a foundation of love and kindness in all our relationships. Through the timeless truths found in John 15, we can draw strength and comfort from our faith, knowing that Jesus is always with us, loving us, and helping us to love others, even when they are unkind.

Chapter 5 – When Your Faith Needs. Stirring – Hebrews 11

This chapter is often called the "Faith Chapter" because it highlights the power and importance of faith through the stories of many biblical figures. It begins with a powerful definition: "Now faith is the substance of things hoped for, the evidence of things not seen" (Hebrews 11:1). This verse explains that faith is believing in something even if we cannot see it yet. It gives us hope and assurance that what we believe in will come to pass. When you need your faith stirred, remembering this definition can help you understand the true essence of faith.

The chapter continues by showing how faith was crucial for many people in the Bible. Hebrews 11:3 states, "Through faith we understand that the worlds were framed by the word of God, so that things which are seen were not made of things which do appear." This reminds us that faith helps us comprehend that God created everything from nothing just by His word. It shows us the incredible power of faith in understanding God's work.

One of the first examples given is Abel, who showed his faith through his offering to God. Hebrews 11:4 says, "By faith Abel offered unto God a more excellent sacrifice than Cain, by which he obtained witness that he was righteous, God testifying of his gifts: and by it he being dead yet speaketh." Abel's faith pleased God, and his story still speaks to us today, reminding us to offer our best to God with faith.

Next, the chapter talks about Enoch, whose faith was so strong that he did not die but was taken directly to heaven. Hebrews 11:5 tells us, "By faith Enoch was translated that he should not see death; and was not found, because God had translated him: for before his translation he had this testimony, that he pleased God." Enoch's life shows us that living a life of faith can bring us closer to God.

Noah is another great example of faith. Hebrews 11:7 states, "By faith Noah, being warned of God of things not seen as yet, moved with fear, prepared an ark to the saving of his house; by the which he condemned the world, and became heir of the righteousness which is by faith." Noah trusted God's warning about the flood and built the ark even though there was no sign of rain. His obedience and faith saved his family and preserved humanity and animals. This story encourages us to trust God's guidance, even when it seems unlikely.

The chapter also highlights Abraham, who is often called the father of faith. Hebrews 11:8 says, "By faith Abraham, when he was called to go out into a place which he should after receive for an inheritance, obeyed; and he went out, not knowing whither he went." Abraham left his home and followed God's call without knowing where he was going. His faith led him to the Promised Land. Later, Hebrews 11:11 mentions Sarah, Abraham's wife, "Through faith also Sara herself received strength to conceive seed, and was delivered of a child when she was past age, because she judged him faithful who had promised." Despite being old, Sarah believed God's promise that she would have a son, Isaac, and her faith was rewarded.

Hebrews 11:17-19 recounts another test of Abraham's faith: "By faith Abraham, when he was tried, offered up Isaac: and he that had received the promises offered up his only begotten son, Of whom it was said, That in Isaac shall thy seed be called: Accounting that God was able to raise him up, even from the dead; from whence also he received him in a figure." Abraham was willing to sacrifice his son Isaac because he believed God could raise him from the dead. This incredible act of faith showed his complete trust in God.

The chapter continues with the faith of Isaac, Jacob, and Joseph. Hebrews 11:20 says, "By faith Isaac blessed Jacob and Esau concerning things to come." Isaac had faith in God's promises for the future of his sons. Hebrews 11:21 states, "By faith Jacob, when he was a dying, blessed both the sons of Joseph; and worshipped, leaning upon the top of his staff." Jacob blessed his grandsons, showing his trust in God's future promises. Hebrews 11:22 recounts Joseph's faith, "By faith Joseph, when he died, made mention of the departing of the children of Israel; and gave commandment concerning his bones." Joseph believed that God would bring the Israelites out of Egypt and wanted his bones taken to the Promised Land, showing his faith in God's promise.

The faith of Moses is also a key part of Hebrews 11. Hebrews 11:23 says, "By faith Moses, when he was born, was hid three months of his parents, because they saw he was a proper child; and they were not afraid of the king's commandment." Moses' parents hid him because they had faith that he was special and trusted God more than the king's orders. Later, Hebrews 11:24-27 recounts Moses' own faith, "By faith Moses, when he was come to years, refused to be called the son of Pharaoh's daughter; Choosing rather to suffer affliction with the people of God, than to enjoy the pleasures of sin for a season; Esteeming the reproach of Christ greater riches than the treasures in Egypt: for he had respect unto the recompense of the reward. By faith he forsook Egypt, not fearing the wrath of the king: for he endured, as seeing him who is invisible." Moses gave up a life of luxury in Egypt to lead the Israelites out of slavery because he believed in God's promises.

The faith of the Israelites during the Exodus is highlighted in Hebrews 11:29-30, "By faith they passed through the Red sea as by dry land: which the Egyptians assaying to do were drowned. By faith the walls of Jericho fell down, after they were compassed about seven days." The Israelites trusted God to lead them through the Red Sea and bring down the walls of Jericho, demonstrating their faith in His power and guidance. The chapter also mentions the faith of Rahab, a woman who protected the Israelite spies in Jericho. Hebrews 11:31 says, "By faith the harlot Rahab perished not with them that believed not, when she had received the spies with peace." Rahab's faith saved her and her family, showing that even those with a difficult past can find salvation through faith.

Hebrews 11 continues to mention many other heroes of faith, including Gideon, Barak, Samson, Jephthah, David, Samuel, and the prophets. Hebrews 11:32-34 states, "And what shall I more say? for the time would fail me to tell of Gedeon, and of Barak, and of Samson, and of Jephthae; of David also, and Samuel, and of the prophets: Who through faith subdued kingdoms, wrought righteousness, obtained promises, stopped the mouths of lions, Quenched the violence of fire, escaped the edge of the sword, out of weakness were made strong, waxed valiant in fight, turned to flight the armies of the aliens." These individuals achieved great things through their faith, demonstrating the incredible power of trusting in God. The chapter also acknowledges the suffering and perseverance of those who kept their faith despite hardships. Hebrews 11:35-38 describes their trials, "Women received their dead raised to life again: and others were tortured, not accepting deliverance; that they might obtain a better resurrection: And others had trial of cruel mockings and scourgings, yea, moreover of bonds and imprisonment: They were stoned, they were sawn asunder, were tempted, were slain with the sword: they wandered about in sheepskins and goatskins; being destitute, afflicted, tormented; (Of whom the world was not worthy:) they wandered in deserts, and in mountains, and in dens and caves of the earth." These verses remind us that faith can carry us through even the most difficult times and that those who suffer for their faith are honored by God.

Hebrews 11 concludes with a powerful message about the ultimate reward of faith. Hebrews 11:39-40 says, "And these all, having obtained a good report through faith, received not the promise: God having provided some better thing for us, that they without us should not be made perfect." This means that all the heroes of faith mentioned in the chapter trusted in God's promises even though they did not see them fulfilled in their lifetimes. They were looking forward to something greater, which we now know is the coming of Jesus Christ and the salvation He offers.

When your faith needs stirring, Hebrews 11 is an excellent chapter to read and reflect on. It reminds us that faith is about trusting in God's promises, even when we cannot see the outcome. The examples of Abel, Enoch, Noah, Abraham, Sarah, Isaac, Jacob, Joseph, Moses, Rahab, and many others show us that faith can lead to great things and carry us through difficult times. Their stories encourage us to stay strong in our faith and trust in God's plan for our lives.

By meditating on the teachings of Hebrews 11, we can find inspiration to strengthen our own faith. Remembering that faith is "the substance of things hoped for, the evidence of things not seen" helps us understand that believing in God's promises, even when they are not immediately visible, is the essence of faith. Reflecting on the lives of the biblical heroes who demonstrated unwavering faith can motivate us to trust in God more deeply and live out our faith with courage and conviction.

In conclusion, Hebrews 11 is a powerful chapter that can stir our faith and inspire us to trust in God more fully. The stories of the heroes of faith remind us that believing in God's promises and staying faithful, even in difficult times, can lead to incredible outcomes. By applying the lessons from Hebrews 11 to our lives, we can strengthen our faith, find encouragement, and draw closer to God. Trusting in God's plan and staying connected to Him through faith can help us navigate life's challenges and achieve great things for His glory. Through the timeless truths found in Hebrews 11, we can find the inspiration and strength we need to keep our faith strong and vibrant.

Chapter 6 – When You Have Sinned – Psalms 51

When you have sinned and feel guilty or ashamed, the Bible offers words of comfort, forgiveness, and guidance to help you seek God's mercy and find a path to repentance. One of the most powerful passages to turn to is Psalms 51. This psalm, written by King David, is a heartfelt prayer for forgiveness and cleansing after he committed a grave sin. It begins with David pleading for God's mercy: "Have mercy upon me, O God, according to thy lovingkindness: according unto the multitude of thy tender mercies blot out my transgressions" (Psalms 51:1). Here, David acknowledges God's great love and compassion and asks for his sins to be erased. This verse reminds us that no matter how much we have sinned, God's mercy is vast and available to us if we sincerely seek it.

In Psalms 51:2, David continues his plea: "Wash me thoroughly from mine iniquity, and cleanse me from my sin." David is asking God to purify him completely from his wrongdoing. This imagery of washing and cleansing shows us that sin can make us feel dirty and tainted, but God's forgiveness can make us clean again. When we have sinned, it is important to ask God to cleanse us and remove the guilt and stain of our sins.

David shows deep sorrow and repentance for his sins in Psalms 51:3-4: "For I acknowledge my transgressions: and my sin is ever before me. Against thee, thee only, have I sinned, and done this evil in thy sight: that thou mightest be justified when thou speakest, and be clear when thou judgest." By acknowledging his sins and understanding that he has wronged God, David takes responsibility for his actions. This teaches us that genuine repentance involves recognizing our sins, admitting them to God, and understanding that our actions have hurt our relationship with Him. Psalms 51:5-6 reveals David's understanding of human nature and God's desire for truth: "Behold, I was shapen in iniquity; and in sin did my mother conceive me. Behold, thou desirest truth in the inward parts: and in the hidden part thou shalt make me to know wisdom." David acknowledges that we are all born with a sinful nature, but he also recognizes that God desires honesty and truth within us. This means being truthful about our sins and seeking God's wisdom to help us live righteously.

In Psalms 51:7, David asks for purification: "Purge me with hyssop, and I shall be clean: wash me, and I shall be whiter than snow." Hyssop was used in ancient rituals for purification, and David uses this imagery to express his desire to be cleansed by God. He believes that God's forgiveness can make him pure and spotless again. This verse reminds us that, through God's mercy, we can be made new and free from the burden of our sins.

David longs for joy and restoration in Psalms 51:8-9: "Make me to hear joy and gladness; that the bones which thou hast broken may rejoice. Hide thy face from my sins, and blot out all mine iniquities." He asks God to restore his joy and to forget his sins. This shows us that repentance not only involves seeking forgiveness but also asking God to renew our spirit and bring back the joy that sin has taken away.

One of the most famous verses in this psalm is Psalms 51:10: "Create in me a clean heart, O God; and renew a right spirit within me." David is asking God to transform him from the inside out, to give him a pure heart and a steadfast spirit. This powerful prayer is a reminder that true repentance involves a desire for inner change and a commitment to living a life that pleases God. When we have sinned, asking God to change our hearts and renew our spirits can help us turn away from sin and live according to His will.

David continues his plea for God's presence and guidance in Psalms 51:11-12: "Cast me not away from thy presence; and take not thy holy spirit from me. Restore unto me the joy of thy salvation; and uphold me with thy free spirit." He fears being separated from God and losing the Holy Spirit's guidance. David asks for the joy of salvation to be restored and for God's Spirit to support him. This shows us the importance of staying close to God and relying on His Spirit to lead us in our daily lives.

In Psalms 51:13, David expresses his desire to help others turn to God: "Then will I teach transgressors thy ways; and sinners shall be converted unto thee." After experiencing God's forgiveness, David wants to share his experience and help others find their way back to God. This verse reminds us that our repentance and transformation can inspire others to seek God's mercy and forgiveness.

David asks for deliverance and praises God in Psalms 51:14-15: "Deliver me from bloodguiltiness, O God, thou God of my salvation: and my tongue shall sing aloud of thy righteousness. O Lord, open thou my lips; and my mouth shall shew forth thy praise." He seeks deliverance from the guilt of his sin and commits to praising God for His righteousness. When we experience God's forgiveness, our natural response should be to praise Him and share His goodness with others.

In Psalms 51:16-17, David acknowledges that God desires a sincere heart rather than mere sacrifices: "For thou desirest not sacrifice; else would I give it: thou delightest not in burnt offering. The sacrifices of God are a broken spirit: a broken and a contrite heart, O God, thou wilt not despise." David understands that God values genuine repentance and a humble heart over ritualistic offerings. This teaches us that true repentance comes from within and involves a sincere desire to change and seek God's forgiveness.

David prays for the well-being of Jerusalem in Psalms 51:18-19: "Do good in thy good pleasure unto Zion: build thou the walls of Jerusalem. Then shalt thou be pleased with the sacrifices of righteousness, with burnt offering and whole burnt offering: then shall they offer bullocks upon thine altar." He asks God to bless and protect the city and its people, showing his concern for the community. This reminds us that our repentance and prayers should extend beyond ourselves to include the well-being of others.

Turning to Psalms 51 when we have sinned can help us understand the importance of genuine repentance and seeking God's mercy. David's heartfelt prayer shows us that no matter how much we have sinned, God's love and forgiveness are always available to us if we come to Him with a sincere and humble heart. By acknowledging our sins, asking for cleansing, and seeking a renewed spirit, we can find thetrengthh to turn away from sin and live a life that honors God.

Reflecting on the verses of Psalms 51 can inspire us to take responsibility for our actions and seek God's forgiveness. The psalm reminds us that God desires truth and sincerity in our hearts and that true repentance involves a commitment to change. By asking God to create a clean heart within us and to renew our spirits, we can find the courage to overcome our sins and grow in our faith.

Applying the lessons from Psalms 51 to our daily lives can help us build a stronger relationship with God. Regularly examining our hearts, confessing our sins, and seeking God's guidance can keep us on the right path and help us avoid falling into sin. By staying connected to God through prayer, reading the Bible, and living according to His teachings, we can experience His mercy and grace in our lives.

In conclusion, Psalms 51 is a powerful and comforting passage to turn to when we have sinned. The heartfelt prayer of King David shows us the importance of genuine repentance, seeking God's forgiveness, and asking for a renewed spirit. By reflecting on these verses and applying their lessons to our lives, we can find the strength to overcome our sins and grow closer to God. Trusting in His mercy and allowing Him to transform our hearts can lead us to a life of righteousness and joy. Through the timeless truths found in Psalms 51, we can experience the depth of God's love and forgiveness and be inspired to live a life that honors Him.

Chapter 7 – When You Worry – Matthew 6:19-34

When you find yourself worrying about the many things in life, the Bible offers guidance and comfort, especially in Matthew 6:19-34. This passage is part of Jesus' Sermon on the Mount, where He teaches about various aspects of faith and life. In this section, Jesus specifically addresses worry and anxiety, providing wisdom on how to trust God for our needs. It starts with Jesus teaching about where we should store our treasures: "Lay not up for yourselves treasures upon earth, where moth and rust doth corrupt, and where thieves break through and steal: But lay up for yourselves treasures in heaven, where neither moth nor rust doth corrupt, and where thieves do not break through nor steal: For where your treasure is, there will your heart be also" (Matthew 6:19-21). This means that we should focus on spiritual wealth rather than material wealth, because earthly treasures are temporary and can be lost, but heavenly treasures are eternal. When we prioritize our relationship with God and spiritual matters, we can find peace and worry less about material things.

Jesus continues by talking about the importance of having a clear and focused mind: "The light of the body is the eye: if therefore thine eye be single, thy whole body shall be full of light. But if thine eye be evil, thy whole body shall be full of darkness. If therefore the light that is in thee be darkness, how great is that darkness!" (Matthew 6:22-23). He is saying that if our focus is on good and righteous things, our whole life will be filled with light and goodness. But if our focus is on evil or material things, our life will be filled with darkness and worry. This teaches us to keep our focus on God and His righteousness to live a life full of light and peace.

Jesus then addresses the issue of serving two masters: "No man can serve two masters: for either he will hate the one, and love the other; or else he will hold to the one, and despise the other. Ye cannot serve God and mammon" (Matthew 6:24). Mammon refers to wealth or material riches. Jesus is teaching that we cannot serve both God and money, as we will end up loving one and hating the other. When we prioritize material wealth over God, it leads to worry and anxiety. Instead, we should serve God wholeheartedly, trusting Him to provide for our needs.

Jesus then speaks directly about worry, saying, "Therefore I say unto you, Take no thought for your life, what ye shall eat, or what ye shall drink; nor yet for your body, what ye shall put on. Is not the life more than meat, and the body than raiment?" (Matthew 6:25). He tells us not to worry about our basic needs like food and clothing, reminding us that life is about more than just these things. By trusting God to take care of our needs, we can focus on more important aspects of life, like our relationship with Him and living according to His will.

Jesus gives an example from nature to illustrate His point: "Behold the fowls of the air: for they sow not, neither do they reap, nor gather into barns; yet your heavenly Father feedeth them. Are ye not much better than they?" (Matthew 6:26). He points out that birds do not worry about their food, yet God provides for them. Since we are more valuable to God than birds, we can trust that He will also provide for us. This example teaches us to have faith in God's provision and care, reducing our worries about material needs.

Jesus continues with another example from nature: "And why take ye thought for raiment? Consider the lilies of the field, how they grow; they toil not, neither do they spin: And yet I say unto you, That even Solomon in all his glory was not arrayed like one of these. Wherefore, if God so clothe the grass of the field, which to day is, and to morrow is cast into the oven, shall he not much more clothe you, O ye of little faith?" (Matthew 6:28-30). He explains that the flowers in the field do not work for their beauty, yet God dresses them more splendidly than even King Solomon. If God takes such care of the flowers, which are temporary, He will surely take care of us. This teaches us to trust in God's care and provision, reminding us that our worries about clothing and other needs are unnecessary.

Jesus then sums up His teaching on worry: "Therefore take no thought, saying, What shall we eat? or, What shall we drink? or, Wherewithal shall we be clothed? (For after all these things do the Gentiles seek:) for your heavenly Father knoweth that ye have need of all these things" (Matthew 6:31-32). He tells us not to worry about our basic needs because God knows what we need and will provide for us. Jesus reminds us that worrying is something those who do not know God do, but as believers, we can trust our heavenly Father to take care of us.

The key verse in this passage is Matthew 6:33: "But seek ye first the kingdom of God, and his righteousness; and all these things shall be added unto you." Jesus instructs us to prioritize seeking God's kingdom and living righteously above all else. When we do this, God promises to provide for our needs. This teaches us that by focusing on our relationship with God and living according to His will, we can trust that He will take care of the rest, alleviating our worries.

Finally, Jesus concludes with a powerful reminder: "Take therefore no thought for the morrow: for the morrow shall take thought for the things of itself. Sufficient unto the day is the evil thereof" (Matthew 6:34). He tells us not to worry about the future, as each day has enough trouble of its own. By focusing on the present and trusting God for the future, we can reduce our worries and live more peacefully.

Turning to Matthew 6:19-34 when we are worried can help us understand the importance of trusting God for our needs and focusing on spiritual matters. Jesus' teachings remind us that God cares for us deeply and knows what we need. By prioritizing our relationship with Him and living according to His will, we can find peace and reduce our worries about material things.

Reflecting on these verses can inspire us to trust in God's provision and care. The examples of the birds and the flowers show us that God takes care of all His creation, and we are even more valuable to Him.

This knowledge can help us let go of our anxieties and rely on God's faithfulness.

Applying the lessons from Matthew 6:19-34 to our daily lives can help us build a stronger faith and reduce worry. By focusing on spiritual treasures rather than material wealth, keeping our minds clear and focused on God, and serving Him wholeheartedly, we can live a life full of peace and trust in God's provision. Regularly seeking God's kingdom and His righteousness can also help us stay aligned with His will and trust that He will take care of our needs.

In conclusion, Matthew 6:19-34 is a powerful passage to turn to when we are worried. Jesus' teachings in this chapter remind us to trust in God's provision, focus on spiritual matters, and prioritize our relationship with Him. By reflecting on these verses and applying their lessons to our lives, we can find peace and reduce our worries about material things. Trusting in God's care and provision, seeking His kingdom, and living according to His will can help us navigate life's challenges with faith and confidence. Through the timeless truths found in Matthew 6:19-34, we can draw strength and comfort from our faith, knowing that God is always with us and will never forsake us.

Chapter 8 – When God Seems Far Away – Psalms 139

When you feel like God is far away and you're alone, the Bible offers comfort and reassurance, especially in Psalms 139. This psalm, written by King David, is a beautiful reminder of God's constant presence and intimate knowledge of us. It begins with David acknowledging God's deep understanding of our lives: "O Lord, thou hast searched me, and known me. Thou knowest my downsitting and mine uprising, thou understandest my thought afar off" (Psalms 139:1-2). These verses tell us that God knows everything about us, from our actions to our thoughts. When we feel distant from God, remembering that He knows us so intimately can be comforting because it means He is always aware of what we are going through.

David continues in Psalms 139:3-4, saying, "Thou compassest my path and my lying down, and art acquainted with all my ways. For there is not a word in my tongue, but, lo, O Lord, thou knowest it altogether." Here, David emphasizes that God is familiar with all our ways and knows our words even before we speak them. This teaches us that God is always with us, understanding every detail of our lives. When we feel like He is far away, it helps to remember that He is always close, knowing our every step and word.

In Psalms 139:5-6, David marvels at God's protection and knowledge: "Thou hast beset me behind and before, and laid thine hand upon me. Such knowledge is too wonderful for me; it is high, I cannot attain unto it." David is in awe of how God surrounds him with His presence and care. The idea that God is both behind and before us, guiding and protecting us, is a powerful reminder that we are never alone. Even when we feel distant from God, His hand is upon us, providing guidance and support.

One of the most comforting parts of this psalm is Psalms 139:7-10, where David speaks about the impossibility of escaping God's presence: "Whither shall I go from thy spirit? or whither shall I flee from thy presence? If I ascend up into heaven, thou art there: if I make my bed in hell, behold, thou art there. If I take the wings of the morning, and dwell in the uttermost parts of the sea; Even there shall thy hand lead me, and thy right hand shall hold me." These verses assure us that no matter where we go, God is there. Whether we are in the highest heavens or the deepest depths, God's presence is with us. This means that even in our darkest moments or when we feel most alone, God is there, holding us with His right hand.

David continues to express his confidence in God's presence in Psalms 139:11-12: "If I say, Surely the darkness shall cover me; even the night shall be light about me. Yea, the darkness hideth not from thee; but the night shineth as the day: the darkness and the light are both alike to thee." These verses tell us that even in the darkest times, God sees us and is with us. Darkness cannot hide us from God because to Him, darkness and light are the same. This teaches us that we can trust God to be with us even when we cannot see a way forward, as His light is always present.

Psalms 139:13-14 speaks about God's creation and care for us from the very beginning: "For thou hast possessed my reins: thou hast covered me in my mother's womb. I will praise thee; for I am fearfully and wonderfully made: marvellous are thy works; and that my soul knoweth right well." David praises God for creating him so wonderfully and for knowing him even before he was born. When we feel far from God, remembering that He made us and knows us from the very start can reassure us of His everlasting presence and care.

David goes on in Psalms 139:15-16, saying, "My substance was not hid from thee, when I was made in secret, and curiously wrought in the lowest parts of the earth. Thine eyes did see my substance, yet being unperfect; and in thy book all my members were written, which in continuance were fashioned, when as yet there was none of them." These verses emphasize that God saw us and knew us even before we were fully formed. Every part of us was known and planned by God. This deep level of care and knowledge reassures us that God has always been with us and will continue to be with us throughout our lives.

In Psalms 139:17-18, David reflects on the preciousness of God's thoughts towards us: "How precious also are thy thoughts unto me, O God! how great is the sum of them! If I should count them, they are more in number than the sand: when I awake, I am still with thee." David marvels at how many thoughts God has for us and how precious they are. This means that God is constantly thinking about us, more than we can even count. When we feel distant from God, knowing that He is always thinking of us can bring great comfort. David then seeks God's guidance in Psalms 139:19-22, asking for protection from the wicked: "Surely thou wilt slay the wicked, O God: depart from me therefore, ye bloody men. For they speak against thee wickedly, and thine enemies take thy name in vain. Do not I hate them, O Lord, that hate thee? and am not I grieved with those that rise up against thee? I hate them with perfect hatred: I count them mine enemies." While these verses speak of David's desire for justice against those who oppose God, they also remind us to seek God's protection and align ourselves with His righteousness.

The psalm concludes with a powerful prayer in Psalms 139:23-24: "Search me, O God, and know my heart: try me, and know my thoughts: And see if there be any wicked way in me, and lead me in the way everlasting." David asks God to examine his heart and thoughts, to reveal any wrong ways in him, and to lead him on the path of righteousness. This shows David's deep desire to be close to God and live according to His will. When we feel far from God, praying this prayer can help us draw closer to Him by asking Him to search our hearts and guide us in the right way.

Turning to Psalms 139 when God seems far away can remind us of His constant presence and deep understanding of us. David's words reassure us that God is always with us, no matter where we go or what we go through. Reflecting on these verses can help us feel God's closeness and care, even when we feel alone.

Applying the lessons from Psalms 139 to our lives can help us build a stronger relationship with God. By acknowledging His intimate knowledge of us, trusting in His constant presence, and seeking His guidance, we can feel more connected to Him. Regularly praying and meditating on these verses can remind us of God's unending care and help us feel His presence more deeply.

In conclusion, Psalms 139 is a powerful passage to turn to when God seems far away. The psalm's beautiful imagery and heartfelt words from David remind us of God's constant presence, deep knowledge of us, and unwavering care. By reflecting on these verses and applying their lessons to our lives, we can find comfort and reassurance in God's closeness. Trusting in His ever-present care and seeking His guidance can help us navigate times of feeling distant from Him. Through the timeless truths found in Psalms 139, we can draw strength and comfort from our faith, knowing that God is always with us and will never forsake us.

Chapter 9 – When You Are Bitter – I Corinthians 13

When you are feeling bitter, it's important to turn to the Bible for guidance and healing, and one of the best chapters for this is I Corinthians 13, often referred to as the "Love Chapter." This chapter, written by the Apostle Paul, provides a beautiful description of love and its importance in our lives, which can help counteract feelings of bitterness. It begins with Paul emphasizing the importance of love above all else: "Though I speak with the tongues of men and of angels, and have not charity, I am become as sounding brass, or a tinkling cymbal" (I Corinthians 13:1). In this verse, "charity" means love. Paul is saying that even if we can speak beautifully and have great knowledge, without love, our words are empty and meaningless. This teaches us that love is the foundation of all our actions and words.

Paul continues in I Corinthians 13:2, "And though I have the gift of prophecy, and understand all mysteries, and all knowledge; and though I have all faith, so that I could remove mountains, and have not charity, I am nothing." This verse tells us that no matter how much we know or how strong our faith is, without love, we are nothing. This helps us understand that love is more important than any other gift or ability we might have. When we feel bitter, remembering that love is the most important thing can help us shift our focus from negative feelings to positive actions.

In I Corinthians 13:3, Paul writes, "And though I bestow all my goods to feed the poor, and though I give my body to be burned, and have not charity, it profiteth me nothing." Here, Paul emphasizes that even the most generous actions are worthless without love. This teaches us that our actions must be motivated by genuine love, not by a desire for recognition or reward. When we feel bitter, focusing on loving others sincerely can help us overcome those negative feelings.

Paul then describes the characteristics of love in I Corinthians 13:4-7: "Charity suffereth long, and is kind; charity envieth not; charity vaunteth not itself, is not puffed up, Doth not behave itself unseemly, seeketh not her own, is not easily provoked, thinketh no evil; Rejoiceth not in iniquity, but rejoiceth in the truth; Beareth all things, believeth all things, hopeth all things, endureth all things." These verses provide a detailed picture of what love looks like in action. Love is patient and kind, it does not envy or boast, it is not proud or rude. Love does not seek its own way, is not easily angered, and keeps no record of wrongs. Love does not delight in evil but rejoices in the truth. Love always protects, trusts, hopes, and perseveres. When we are bitter, reflecting on these qualities can help us see how we can change our behavior and attitudes to be more loving and less bitter.

I Corinthians 13:8 states, "Charity never faileth: but whether there be prophecies, they shall fail; whether there be tongues, they shall cease; whether there be knowledge, it shall vanish away." This verse tells us that love never fails, even when other things pass away. Prophecies, languages, and knowledge are temporary, but love is eternal. This teaches us the enduring power of love and its importance in our lives. When we feel bitter, focusing on the eternal nature of love can help us find stability and peace.

Paul continues in I Corinthians 13:9-10, "For we know in part, and we prophesy in part. But when that which is perfect is come, then that which is in part shall be done away." These verses remind us that our knowledge and understanding are limited, but when perfection comes, these partial things will disappear. This teaches us to be humble and recognize that we do not have all the answers. When we are bitter, accepting our limitations and focusing on love can help us find peace.

In I Corinthians 13:11, Paul writes, "When I was a child, I spake as a child, I understood as a child, I thought as a child: but when I became a man, I put away childish things." This verse encourages us to grow and mature in our understanding and actions. Childish ways of thinking and acting, such as holding onto bitterness, should be put aside as we grow in love. This teaches us that maturity involves letting go of negative feelings and embracing love.

Paul continues in I Corinthians 13:12, "For now we see through a glass, darkly; but then face to face: now I know in part; but then shall I know even as also I am known." This verse tells us that our current understanding is limited, like looking through a dark glass, but one day we will see clearly and understand fully. This reminds us to be patient and trust that our understanding will grow. When we feel bitter, trusting that we will eventually see things clearly can help us let go of our negative feelings.

I Corinthians 13:13 concludes with a powerful statement: "And now abideth faith, hope, charity, these three; but the greatest of these is charity." This verse tells us that faith, hope, and love are the three most important things, but love is the greatest. This teaches us the supreme importance of love in our lives. When we are bitter, focusing on love as the greatest virtue can help us transform our feelings and actions.

Turning to I Corinthians 13 when we feel bitter can remind us of the importance of love and help us find a path to healing. Paul's words about the qualities of love and its enduring nature provide a powerful antidote to bitterness. Reflecting on these verses can inspire us to cultivate love in our hearts and actions, even when we are struggling with negative emotions.

Applying the lessons from I Corinthians 13 to our lives can help us build stronger, more loving relationships. By practicing patience, kindness, and humility, and by letting go of envy, pride, and anger, we can create a more positive and loving environment for ourselves and those around us. Regularly reflecting on these verses and striving to embody the qualities of love can help us overcome bitterness and live a more fulfilling and peaceful life.

In conclusion, I Corinthians 13 is a powerful passage to turn to when you are feeling bitter. The chapter's beautiful description of love and its importance provides a roadmap for transforming negative emotions into positive actions. By reflecting on these verses and applying their lessons to our lives, we can find healing and strength in love. Trusting in the enduring power of love and striving to embody its qualities can help us navigate life's challenges with grace and compassion. Through the timeless truths found in I Corinthians 13, we can draw strength and comfort from our faith, knowing that love is the greatest virtue and the key to overcoming bitterness.

Chapter 10 – When You Are In Danger – Psalms 91

When you feel in danger, scared, or threatened, turning to the Bible for comfort and protection can be very helpful, and Psalms 91 is one of the best passages to read. This psalm, attributed to Moses or David, is a powerful reminder of God's protection and care for those who trust in Him. It begins with, "He that dwelleth in the secret place of the most High shall abide under the shadow of the Almighty" (Psalms 91:1). This verse tells us that those who live in close relationship with God are under His protection, just like being in the safe shadow of a mighty fortress. When we are in danger, remembering that we are under God's protection can give us a sense of peace and security.

Psalms 91:2 continues, "I will say of the Lord, He is my refuge and my fortress: my God; in him will I trust." Here, the psalmist declares that God is his safe place and strong protector, and he puts his trust in Him. This teaches us to trust God completely, especially when we are in danger. By declaring our trust in God's protection, we reinforce our faith and remind ourselves that He is our refuge.

In Psalms 91:3, it says, "Surely he shall deliver thee from the snare of the fowler, and from the noisome pestilence." This verse promises that God will save us from hidden traps and deadly diseases. This teaches us that God can protect us from dangers we cannot see and from things that threaten our health. When we feel in danger, trusting in God's promise to deliver us from these threats can bring us comfort.

Psalms 91:4 provides a comforting image: "He shall cover thee with his feathers, and under his wings shalt thou trust: his truth shall be thy shield and buckler." This verse uses the picture of a bird protecting its young with its wings to show how God shields us. It also tells us that God's truth is our protection, like a shield in battle. This teaches us that

God's protection is both tender and strong, and His truth is a powerful defense against danger.

In Psalms 91:5-6, it says, "Thou shalt not be afraid for the terror by night; nor for the arrow that flieth by day; Nor for the pestilence that walketh in darkness; nor for the destruction that wasteth at noonday." These verses tell us not to fear dangers that come at any time—whether at night or during the day, whether hidden or obvious. This teaches us that with God's protection, we do not need to live in fear of any kind of danger.

Psalms 91:7 offers more reassurance: "A thousand shall fall at thy side, and ten thousand at thy right hand; but it shall not come nigh thee." This verse means that even if many people around us fall to danger, it will not touch us. This teaches us that God's protection can keep us safe even when we are surrounded by threats. When we feel in danger, remembering this promise can help us stay calm and trust in God's protection. In Psalms 91:8-10, it says, "Only with thine eyes shalt thou behold and see the reward of the wicked. Because thou hast made the Lord, which is my refuge, even the most High, thy habitation; There shall no evil befall thee, neither shall any plague come nigh thy dwelling." These verses tell us that because we have made God our safe place, we will only see the punishment of the wicked and will not be harmed by evil or disease. This teaches us the importance of staying close to God and making Him our refuge, trusting that He will protect us from harm.

Psalms 91:11-12 explains how God protects us: "For he shall give his angels charge over thee, to keep thee in all thy ways. They shall bear thee up in their hands, lest thou dash thy foot against a stone." These verses tell us that God sends His angels to watch over us and keep us from harm. This teaches us that we are never alone, even in danger, because God's angels are there to protect us. When we feel threatened, remembering that God has sent His angels to guard us can provide a great sense of comfort and security.

In Psalms 91:13, it says, "Thou shalt tread upon the lion and adder: the young lion and the dragon shalt thou trample under feet." This verse tells us that we will overcome dangerous animals and threats, symbolizing that with God's help, we can defeat powerful enemies and dangers. This teaches us that with God's protection, we have the strength and courage to face and overcome any danger.

Psalms 91:14-16 are God's promises to those who love Him: "Because he hath set his love upon me, therefore will I deliver him: I will set him on high, because he hath known my name. He shall call upon me, and I will answer him: I will be with him in trouble; I will deliver him, and honour him. With long life will I satisfy him, and shew him my salvation." These verses tell us that because we love God and know His name, He will protect us, answer our prayers, be with us in trouble, deliver us, honor us, give us long life, and show us His salvation. This teaches us that a loving relationship with God brings His protection and blessings.

Turning to Psalms 91 when we are in danger can remind us of God's constant protection and care. The imagery of God as a refuge, a fortress, and a protective bird covering us with His wings provides a powerful sense of security. Reflecting on these verses can help us feel God's presence and trust in His promises to keep us safe.

Applying the lessons from Psalms 91 to our lives can help us build a stronger faith and reduce fear. By declaring our trust in God, seeking His protection, and remembering His promises, we can face danger with confidence. Regularly reading and meditating on these verses can strengthen our faith and remind us of God's unfailing protection.

In conclusion, Psalms 91 is a powerful passage to turn to when you are in danger. The psalm's vivid imagery and comforting words remind us of God's constant protection and care. By reflecting on these verses and applying their lessons to our lives, we can find peace and security in God's presence. Trusting in His promises and seeking His protection can help us navigate dangerous situations with faith and confidence. Through the timeless truths found in Psalms 91, we can draw strength and comfort from our faith, knowing that God is always with us and will never forsake us.

Chapter 11 – If Your Wallet Is Empty – Psalms 37

When you are worried about money and your wallet is empty, turning to the Bible for guidance and comfort can provide much-needed reassurance. Psalms 37 is a powerful chapter that addresses trusting in God, especially when facing financial difficulties. This psalm, written by David, encourages us to focus on God's faithfulness and His provision rather than our worries about material needs. It begins with, "Fret not thyself because of evildoers, neither be thou envious against the workers of iniquity" (Psalms 37:1). This verse tells us not to worry about those who do wrong or envy people who seem to prosper by doing bad things. When we are struggling with money, it is important to keep our focus on God and not compare ourselves to others.

David continues in Psalms 37:3-4, "Trust in the Lord, and do good; so shalt thou dwell in the land, and verily thou shalt be fed. Delight thyself also in the Lord; and he shall give thee the desires of thine heart." These verses teach us to trust in God and continue doing good, knowing that He will take care of our needs. By finding joy in our relationship with God, we can trust that He will provide for us. When our wallet is empty, remembering to trust in God's provision can help us feel more secure.

In Psalms 37:5-6, David writes, "Commit thy way unto the Lord; trust also in him; and he shall bring it to pass. And he shall bring forth thy righteousness as the light, and thy judgment as the noonday." This means we should commit our lives and our plans to God, trusting that He will take care of us and bring about good outcomes. When we are worried about money, committing our worries and needs to God can help us find peace and assurance that He is in control.

Psalms 37:7 advises, "Rest in the Lord, and wait patiently for him: fret not thyself because of him who prospereth in his way, because of the man who bringeth wicked devices to pass." This verse teaches us to be patient and rest in God, not to worry about others who seem to succeed through wrongdoing. Patience and trust in God's timing are crucial when we face financial struggles, as they remind us that God knows our needs and will provide in His perfect timing.

David continues to encourage trust in God with Psalms 37:8-9, "Cease from anger, and forsake wrath: fret not thyself in any wise to do evil. For evildoers shall be cut off: but those that wait upon the Lord, they shall inherit the earth." These verses tell us to avoid anger and wrongdoing, as those who do wrong will face consequences, but those who wait on God will receive His blessings. This teaches us the importance of maintaining a righteous and patient attitude, even when we are facing financial difficulties.

Psalms 37:16-17 provides perspective on wealth: "A little that a righteous man hath is better than the riches of many wicked. For the arms of the wicked shall be broken: but the Lord upholdeth the righteous." These verses remind us that even a small amount in the hands of a righteous person is better than the wealth of those who do wrong because God supports the righteous. When our wallet is empty, valuing what we have and trusting in God's support can help us feel more content.

In Psalms 37:18-19, David writes, "The Lord knoweth the days of the upright: and their inheritance shall be for ever. They shall not be ashamed in the evil time: and in the days of famine they shall be satisfied." This means that God knows the lives of the righteous and will provide for them even in difficult times. These verses reassure us that God is aware of our needs and will take care of us, even when resources are scarce.

Psalms 37:23-24 offers further comfort: "The steps of a good man are ordered by the Lord: and he delighteth in his way. Though he fall, he shall not be utterly cast down: for the Lord upholdeth him with his hand." These verses tell us that God guides the path of those who follow

Him and supports them even when they face difficulties. Trusting in God's guidance and support can help us navigate financial challenges without fear of falling.

David continues with Psalms 37:25-26, sharing his own experience: "I have been young, and now am old; yet have I not seen the righteous forsaken, nor his seed begging bread. He is ever merciful, and lendeth; and his seed is blessed." David reassures us that throughout his life, he has seen God provide for the righteous, ensuring they are never left in need. This teaches us that God's provision is faithful and reliable, encouraging us to trust in His mercy and generosity.

Psalms 37:28-29 promises protection for the righteous: "For the Lord loveth judgment, and forsaketh not his saints; they are preserved for ever: but the seed of the wicked shall be cut off. The righteous shall inherit the land, and dwell therein for ever." These verses remind us that God loves justice and will never abandon His faithful followers, ensuring their safety and provision. When we face financial struggles, trusting in God's justice and care can help us feel secure.

In Psalms 37:30-31, David highlights the importance of wisdom and God's law: "The mouth of the righteous speaketh wisdom, and his tongue talketh of judgment. The law of his God is in his heart; none of his steps shall slide." These verses teach us that by following God's wisdom and keeping His law in our hearts, we can find stability and avoid making poor decisions. When our wallet is empty, seeking God's wisdom can help us manage our resources wisely.

Psalms 37:34 encourages patience and trust: "Wait on the Lord, and keep his way, and he shall exalt thee to inherit the land: when the wicked are cut off, thou shalt see it." This verse reminds us to be patient and continue following God's ways, trusting that He will lift us up and provide for us. Patience and faithfulness in following God are key to experiencing His provision.

David continues with Psalms 37:37-38, contrasting the fate of the righteous and the wicked: "Mark the perfect man, and behold the upright: for the end of that man is peace. But the transgressors shall be destroyed together: the end of the wicked shall be cut off." These verses teach us that those who live righteously will find peace, while those who do wrong will face destruction. When we are struggling financially, maintaining righteousness and trusting in God's justice can bring us peace.

Psalms 37:39-40 concludes with a promise of deliverance: "But the salvation of the righteous is of the Lord: he is their strength in the time of trouble. And the Lord shall help them, and deliver them: he shall deliver them from the wicked, and save them, because they trust in him." These verses reassure us that God is our strength and salvation, especially in times of trouble, and He will deliver and save those who trust in Him. When our wallet is empty, trusting in God's deliverance and strength can help us find hope and courage.

Turning to Psalms 37 when our wallet is empty can remind us of God's faithfulness and provision. David's words encourage us to trust in God's timing, avoid envy and wrongdoing, and focus on living righteously. Reflecting on these verses can help us find peace and security in God's promises.

Applying the lessons from Psalms 37 to our lives can help us build a stronger faith and manage financial difficulties wisely. By trusting in God's provision, seeking His wisdom, and maintaining patience and righteousness, we can navigate financial challenges with confidence. Regularly reading and meditating on these verses can strengthen our faith and remind us of God's unfailing support.

In conclusion, Psalms 37 is a powerful passage to turn to when your wallet is empty. The psalm's encouraging words and timeless truths remind us of God's faithfulness and provision. By reflecting on these verses and applying their lessons to our lives, we can find peace and security in God's care. Trusting in His promises, seeking His wisdom, and living righteously can help us navigate financial struggles with faith and confidence. Through the timeless truths found in Psalms 37, we can draw strength and comfort from our faith, knowing that God is always with us and will never forsake us.

Chapter 12 – Christian Assurance – Romans 8:1-30

When you need assurance in your Christian faith, turning to the Bible for guidance and comfort can be very helpful, and Romans 8:1-30 is one of the most reassuring passages. Written by the Apostle Paul, this chapter reminds us of the security and hope we have in Christ. It begins with a powerful statement: "There is therefore now no condemnation to them which are in Christ Jesus, who walk not after the flesh, but after the Spirit" (Romans 8:1). This verse tells us that if we are in Christ Jesus and live according to the Spirit, we are not condemned. This means that through Jesus, we are forgiven and free from the guilt and punishment of sin. When we need assurance, remembering that we are no longer condemned because of Christ can give us great peace and confidence.

Paul continues in Romans 8:2, "For the law of the Spirit of life in Christ Jesus hath made me free from the law of sin and death." This verse tells us that the Spirit of life in Christ has freed us from the power of sin and death. We no longer have to be bound by our sinful nature, because Jesus has given us new life through His Spirit. This teaches us that we are liberated from the old ways of sin and death, and we can live a new life in the Spirit.

In Romans 8:3-4, Paul explains how this freedom was achieved: "For what the law could not do, in that it was weak through the flesh, God sending his own Son in the likeness of sinful flesh, and for sin, condemned sin in the flesh: That the righteousness of the law might be fulfilled in us, who walk not after the flesh, but after the Spirit." These verses tell us that the law was unable to save us because of our sinful nature, but God sent His Son, Jesus, to take on human form and condemn sin in His flesh. By doing this, Jesus fulfilled the law's requirements, allowing us to live righteously by following the Spirit. This reassures us that through Jesus, we can meet God's standards and live a life pleasing to Him.

Paul continues in Romans 8:5-6, "For they that are after the flesh do mind the things of the flesh; but they that are after the Spirit the things of the Spirit. For to be carnally minded is death; but to be spiritually minded is life and peace." These verses teach us that focusing on the desires of the flesh leads to death, but focusing on the Spirit brings life and peace. When we need assurance, choosing to focus on spiritual things rather than worldly desires can help us experience the life and peace that come from God.

In Romans 8:7-8, Paul emphasizes the conflict between the flesh and the Spirit: "Because the carnal mind is enmity against God: for it is not subject to the law of God, neither indeed can be. So then they that are in the flesh cannot please God." These verses tell us that a mind focused on the flesh is hostile to God and cannot please Him. This teaches us the importance of living according to the Spirit, as this is the only way to truly please God.

Romans 8:9 provides reassurance to believers: "But ye are not in the flesh, but in the Spirit, if so be that the Spirit of God dwell in you. Now if any man have not the Spirit of Christ, he is none of his." This verse tells us that if the Spirit of God lives in us, we are not controlled by the flesh but by the Spirit. This reassures us that as believers, we belong to Christ because His Spirit lives in us.

Paul continues in Romans 8:10-11, "And if Christ be in you, the body is dead because of sin; but the Spirit is life because of righteousness. But if the Spirit of him that raised up Jesus from the dead dwell in you, he that raised up Christ from the dead shall also quicken your mortal bodies by his Spirit that dwelleth in you." These verses tell us that if Christ lives in us, our sinful nature is dead, and the Spirit gives us life because of righteousness. Moreover, the same Spirit that raised Jesus from the dead will also give life to our mortal bodies. This reassures us that we have new life in Christ and that His Spirit will sustain us.

In Romans 8:12-13, Paul reminds us of our responsibility: "Therefore, brethren, we are debtors, not to the flesh, to live after the flesh. For if ye live after the flesh, ye shall die: but if ye through the Spirit do mortify the deeds of the body, ye shall live." These verses teach us that we are not obligated to live according to the flesh but should put to death the deeds of the body through the Spirit to experience true life. This reassures us that we have the power to overcome our sinful nature through the Spirit.

Romans 8:14-15 provides further reassurance of our identity in Christ: "For as many as are led by the Spirit of God, they are the sons of God. For ye have not received the spirit of bondage again to fear; but ye have received the Spirit of adoption, whereby we cry, Abba, Father." These verses tell us that those who are led by the Spirit are children of God, and we have received the Spirit of adoption, allowing us to call God our Father. This reassures us that we are part of God's family and can approach Him with the confidence of beloved children.

Paul continues in Romans 8:16-17, "The Spirit itself beareth witness with our spirit, that we are the children of God: And if children, then heirs; heirs of God, and joint-heirs with Christ; if so be that we suffer with him, that we may be also glorified together." These verses tell us that the Spirit confirms that we are God's children and heirs, sharing in the inheritance with Christ. This teaches us that we have a glorious future with Christ, even if we face suffering now. When we need assurance, remembering that we are heirs with Christ can give us hope and confidence.

In Romans 8:18, Paul offers a perspective on suffering: "For I reckon that the sufferings of this present time are not worthy to be compared with the glory which shall be revealed in us." This verse tells us that our current sufferings are insignificant compared to the future glory that will be revealed in us. This teaches us to focus on the eternal hope we have in Christ, which far outweighs our present difficulties.

Paul continues with a description of creation's longing for redemption in Romans 8:19-21: "For the earnest expectation of the creature waiteth for the manifestation of the sons of God. For the creature was made subject to vanity, not willingly, but by reason of him who hath subjected the same in hope, Because the creature itself also shall be delivered from the bondage of corruption into the glorious liberty of the children of God." These verses tell us that creation eagerly waits for the revealing of God's children and will be liberated from its current state of decay. This reassures us that God's redemption plan includes all of creation and that we have a part in that glorious future.

In Romans 8:22-23, Paul explains the current state of creation and believers: "For we know that the whole creation groaneth and travaileth in pain together until now. And not only they, but ourselves also, which have the firstfruits of the Spirit, even we ourselves groan within ourselves, waiting for the adoption, to wit, the redemption of our body." These verses tell us that both creation and believers groan in anticipation of the full realization of our redemption. This teaches us to be patient and hopeful as we await the completion of God's redemptive work.

Romans 8:24-25 emphasizes hope: "For we are saved by hope: but hope that is seen is not hope: for what a man seeth, why doth he yet hope for? But if we hope for that we see not, then do we with patience wait for it." These verses tell us that our salvation is characterized by hope in what is not yet seen, and we must wait patiently for its fulfillment. This reassures us that our faith is rooted in a confident expectation of God's promises.

In Romans 8:26-27, Paul provides reassurance of the Spirit's help: "Likewise the Spirit also helpeth our infirmities: for we know not what we should pray for as we ought: but the Spirit itself maketh intercession for us with groanings which cannot be uttered. And he that searcheth the hearts knoweth what is the mind of the Spirit, because he maketh intercession for the saints according to the will of God." These verses tell us that the Spirit helps us in our weakness, interceding for us with groanings that words cannot express. This teaches us that even when we do not know how to pray, the Spirit prays for us according to God's will, giving us assurance that our prayers are heard.

Romans 8:28 provides one of the most comforting promises in the Bible: "And we know that all things work together for good to them that love God, to them who are the called according to his purpose." This verse tells us that God works all things together for the good of those who love Him and are called according to His purpose. This reassures us that even in difficult circumstances, God is working for our good and His glory.

Paul continues in Romans 8:29-30, "For whom he did foreknow, he also did predestinate to be conformed to the image of his Son, that he might be the firstborn among many brethren. Moreover whom he did predestinate, them he also called: and whom he called, them he also justified: and whom he justified, them he also glorified." These verses tell us that God has a sovereign plan for our lives, from foreknowing and predestining us to calling, justifying, and glorifying us. This teaches us that our entire salvation journey is part of God's divine plan, providing us with assurance and confidence in His perfect work.

Turning to Romans 8:1-30 when we need assurance can remind us of God's unfailing love and His perfect plan for our lives. Paul's words reassure us that we are no longer condemned, that we are children and heirs of God, and that the Spirit helps us in our weaknesses. Reflecting on these verses can help us find peace and security in God's promises.

Applying the lessons from Romans 8:1-30 to our lives can help us build a stronger faith and experience the fullness of God's love and assurance. By focusing on the Spirit, trusting in God's promises, and remembering our identity in Christ, we can navigate life's challenges with confidence. Regularly reading and meditating on these verses can strengthen our faith and remind us of God's unfailing support.

In conclusion, Romans 8:1-30 is a powerful passage to turn to when you need Christian assurance. The chapter's encouraging words and timeless truths remind us of God's faithfulness and His perfect plan for our lives. By reflecting on these verses and applying their lessons to our lives, we can find peace and security in God's love. Trusting in His promises, seeking the guidance of the Spirit, and embracing our identity as children of God can help us navigate life's challenges with faith and confidence. Through the timeless truths found in Romans 8:1-30, we can draw strength and comfort from our faith, knowing that God is always with us and will never forsake us.

Chapter 13 – When Your Prayers Grow Selfish – Psalms 67

When you notice your prayers becoming selfish, it's helpful to turn to the Bible for guidance on how to pray in a way that honors God and benefits others. Psalms 67 is an excellent chapter for this, as it focuses on seeking God's blessings not just for oneself but for the entire world, so that God's ways and salvation can be known everywhere. The psalm starts with a humble plea for God's grace and blessings: "God be merciful unto us, and bless us; and cause his face to shine upon us; Selah" (Psalms 67:1). This verse shows that while it is good to ask for God's mercy and blessings, it is also important to seek His presence in our lives. Asking for God's face to shine upon us means we are seeking His favor and guidance, which leads us away from selfishness and toward a deeper relationship with Him.

The purpose of these blessings is made clear in Psalms 67:2: "That thy way may be known upon earth, thy saving health among all nations." This verse teaches us that the ultimate reason for asking for God's blessings is so that His ways can be known throughout the earth and His salvation can reach all nations. When our prayers become self-centered, this verse reminds us to think beyond our own needs and desires, and to focus on the greater goal of spreading God's message of love and salvation to others.

In Psalms 67:3, the psalmist says, "Let the people praise thee, O God; let all the people praise thee." This verse is a call for universal praise to God. It shifts the focus from ourselves to a desire for everyone to recognize and worship God. When our prayers grow selfish, including prayers for all people to praise God can help us reorient our hearts towards a more God-centered perspective.

Psalms 67:4 continues this theme: "O let the nations be glad and sing for joy: for thou shalt judge the people righteously, and govern the nations upon earth. Selah." This verse expresses a desire for all nations to experience joy and gladness because of God's righteous judgment and governance. It teaches us that God's rule brings justice and peace, and our prayers should reflect a longing for all people to experience the joy of living under His righteous rule. When we focus on the well-being and salvation of others, our prayers become more aligned with God's heart.

In Psalms 67:5, the psalmist repeats the call for universal praise: "Let the people praise thee, O God; let all the people praise thee." Repetition in this verse emphasizes the importance of this request. This teaches us that one of the highest aims of our prayers should be the glorification of God by all people. When we find our prayers focusing too much on ourselves, praying for God's praise to spread can help redirect our hearts toward His glory.

Psalms 67:6-7 concludes with a vision of God's blessings bringing abundance and reverence: "Then shall the earth yield her increase; and God, even our own God, shall bless us. God shall bless us; and all the ends of the earth shall fear him." These verses tell us that when God blesses us, it results in the earth's increase and leads to reverence for God among all people. This teaches us that God's blessings are not just for our comfort but are meant to demonstrate His goodness and power to the world, leading others to respect and worship Him. When our prayers become selfish, remembering that God's blessings have a greater purpose can help us pray with a broader perspective.

Reflecting on the verses of Psalms 67 can inspire us to pray more selflessly, asking for God's mercy and blessings with the intention of sharing His love and glory with others. By focusing on the well-being and salvation of people around us and around the world, we align our prayers with God's heart and purpose. Applying the lessons from Psalms 67 to our prayer life can help us develop a more God-centered approach to prayer. By seeking God's blessings with the desire for His ways to be known and His salvation to spread, we can pray with a broader vision that goes beyond our own needs. Regularly praying for others to know and praise God can transform our prayers from self-centered requests to powerful petitions that seek to advance God's kingdom.

Turning to Psalms 67 when our prayers grow selfish can remind us of the importance of seeking God's blessings for the sake of His glory and the salvation of others. The psalm encourages us to focus on the spread of God's ways and the praise of all people, shifting our attention from ourselves to God's greater plan. By seeking God's blessings with the desire for His ways to be known and His salvation to spread, we can pray with a broader vision that goes beyond our own needs. Regularly praying for others to know and praise God can transform our prayers from self-centered requests to powerful petitions that seek to advance God's kingdom. In conclusion, Psalms 67 is a powerful passage to turn to when your prayers grow selfish. The psalm's focus on God's mercy, blessings, and the spread of His ways and salvation reminds us to pray with a broader vision that honors God and seeks the well-being of others. By reflecting on these verses and applying their lessons to our prayer life, we can find new depth and purpose in our prayers. Trusting in God's desire to bless us for the sake of His glory and the salvation of people around the world can help us develop a more selfless and God-honoring approach to prayer. Through the timeless truths found in Psalms 67, we can draw strength and comfort from our faith, knowing that our prayers, when aligned with God's heart, can have a powerful impact on our lives and the lives of others.

Chapter 14 – For A Great Opportunity – Isaiah 55

When you face a great opportunity and seek guidance, the Bible offers wisdom and encouragement, especially in Isaiah 55. This chapter is a beautiful invitation from God, calling people to come to Him, receive His blessings, and embrace His ways. It begins with an open invitation: "Ho, every one that thirsteth, come ye to the waters, and he that hath no money; come ye, buy, and eat; yea, come, buy wine and milk without money and without price" (Isaiah 55:1). This verse tells us that God's blessings are available to everyone, regardless of their means. When you face a great opportunity, remembering that God's provision is freely given can help you approach it with confidence, knowing that He will provide what you need.

Isaiah 55:2 continues with a question and a promise: "Wherefore do ye spend money for that which is not bread? and your labour for that which satisfieth not? hearken diligently unto me, and eat ye that which is good, and let your soul delight itself in fatness." This verse encourages us to focus on what truly satisfies and brings joy to our souls. When you have a great opportunity, it's important to prioritize what will bring lasting fulfillment rather than temporary gain. By listening to God's guidance, you can make choices that lead to true satisfaction.

In Isaiah 55:3, God extends His promise further: "Incline your ear, and come unto me: hear, and your soul shall live; and I will make an everlasting covenant with you, even the sure mercies of David." This verse invites us to listen to God and enter into a covenant with Him, promising life and steadfast love. When you face a significant opportunity, seeking God's voice and committing to His ways can ensure that your decisions are grounded in His eternal promises.

Isaiah 55:4-5 highlights the influence and reach of God's call: "Behold, I have given him for a witness to the people, a leader and commander to the people. Behold, thou shalt call a nation that thou knowest not, and nations that knew not thee shall run unto thee because of the Lord thy God, and for the Holy One of Israel; for he hath glorified thee." These verses speak of a leader who will draw nations to God. When you have a great opportunity, recognizing that your actions can have a far-reaching impact can motivate you to seek God's guidance and use the opportunity to glorify Him.

Isaiah 55:6-7 urges us to seek God and turn from our ways: "Seek ye the Lord while he may be found, call ye upon him while he is near: Let the wicked forsake his way, and the unrighteous man his thoughts: and let him return unto the Lord, and he will have mercy upon him; and to our God, for he will abundantly pardon." These verses encourage us to seek God earnestly and repent from any wrongdoings. When you face a great opportunity, it's crucial to approach it with a pure heart, seeking God's presence and His mercy, knowing that He will forgive and guide you.

Isaiah 55:8-9 reminds us of the vast difference between our thoughts and God's thoughts: "For my thoughts are not your thoughts, neither are your ways my ways, saith the Lord. For as the heavens are higher than the earth, so are my ways higher than your ways, and my thoughts than your thoughts." These verses teach us that God's wisdom and plans are far beyond our understanding. When you encounter a great opportunity, trusting in God's superior wisdom and seeking His direction can lead you to outcomes far greater than you could imagine on your own.

In Isaiah 55:10-11, God compares His word to rain and snow that nourish the earth: "For as the rain cometh down, and the snow from heaven, and returneth not thither, but watereth the earth, and maketh it bring forth and bud, that it may give seed to the sower, and bread to the eater: So shall my word be that goeth forth out of my mouth: it shall not return unto me void, but it shall accomplish that which I please, and it shall prosper in the thing whereto I sent it." These verses assure us that God's word is powerful and effective, achieving His purposes. When you face a great opportunity, relying on God's word and trusting in its power can give you confidence that His plans will be fulfilled in your life.

Isaiah 55:12-13 describes the joyful and transformative effects of following God's ways: "For ye shall go out with joy, and be led forth with peace: the mountains and the hills shall break forth before you into singing, and all the trees of the field shall clap their hands. Instead of the thorn shall come up the fir tree, and instead of the brier shall come up the myrtle tree: and it shall be to the Lord for a name, for an everlasting sign that shall not be cut off." These verses paint a picture of joy, peace, and transformation that come from embracing God's guidance. When you have a great opportunity, seeking God's direction can lead to profound joy and positive change, both in your life and in the lives of others.

Turning to Isaiah 55 when you face a great opportunity can remind you of the importance of seeking God's guidance, trusting in His provision, and focusing on His eternal promises. The chapter encourages us to prioritize what truly satisfies, listen to God's voice, and recognize the far-reaching impact of our actions when aligned with His will.

Reflecting on the verses of Isaiah 55 can inspire you to approach opportunities with a God-centered perspective, seeking His wisdom and trusting in His plans. By prioritizing your relationship with God and committing to His ways, you can navigate opportunities in a way that brings lasting fulfillment and glorifies Him.

Applying the lessons from Isaiah 55 to your life can help you make wise decisions and embrace opportunities with confidence and faith. By seeking God's guidance, trusting in His word, and recognizing the transformative power of His presence, you can approach opportunities with a heart full of hope and a spirit ready to follow His lead.

In conclusion, Isaiah 55 is a powerful chapter to turn to when you face a great opportunity. The chapter's encouraging words and timeless truths remind us of God's faithfulness, His superior wisdom, and the joy that comes from following His ways. By reflecting on these verses and applying their lessons to your life, you can find confidence and guidance in God's presence. Trusting in His provision, seeking His direction, and embracing His promises can help you navigate opportunities with faith and assurance. Through the timeless truths found in Isaiah 55, you can draw strength and comfort from your faith, knowing that God's word will accomplish His purposes in your life and bring about joy and transformation.

Chapter 15 – When You Leave To Travel – Psalms 123

When you are about to leave for a journey and seek guidance, protection, and peace, turning to the Bible can provide comfort and reassurance. Psalms 123 is a brief but powerful chapter that focuses on looking to God for mercy and help. This psalm, written as a song of ascents, reflects the Israelites' reliance on God during their travels and challenges. It begins with a humble plea, "Unto thee lift I up mine eyes, O thou that dwellest in the heavens" (Psalms 123:1). This verse encourages us to look up to God, who is in heaven, recognizing His sovereign power and our dependence on Him. When you are preparing to travel, lifting your eyes to God and acknowledging His control over your journey can provide a sense of peace and trust in His protection.

Psalms 123:2 continues with a vivid metaphor of dependence, "Behold, as the eyes of servants look unto the hand of their masters, and as the eyes of a maiden unto the hand of her mistress; so our eyes wait upon the Lord our God, until that he have mercy upon us." This verse highlights the trust and dependence that servants have on their masters, and it parallels our dependence on God. Just as servants look to their masters for provision and direction, we look to God for guidance and mercy. When you embark on a journey, recognizing this dependence and seeking God's direction can help you navigate your travels with confidence.

In Psalms 123:3, the psalmist makes a heartfelt plea for mercy, "Have mercy upon us, O Lord, have mercy upon us: for we are exceedingly filled with contempt." This verse shows a deep sense of need for God's mercy, reflecting a humble heart that acknowledges human limitations and the challenges faced. When traveling, it is important to ask for God's mercy and protection, understanding that we may encounter difficulties and need His help to overcome them.

The psalm concludes with a reflection on the scorn and contempt faced by the psalmist and the community, "Our soul is exceedingly filled with the scorning of those that are at ease, and with the contempt of the proud" (Psalms 123:4). This verse acknowledges the reality of facing disdain and arrogance from others, and it serves as a reminder that we are not alone in our struggles. When you travel, you may encounter challenges, but knowing that others have faced similar difficulties and sought God's help can provide comfort and strength.

Turning to Psalms 123 when you leave to travel can remind you of the importance of looking to God for guidance, mercy, and protection. The chapter encourages a humble dependence on God, recognizing His sovereignty and our need for His help. Reflecting on these verses can help you feel God's presence and trust in His care throughout your journey.

Reflecting on the verses of Psalms 123 can inspire you to approach your travels with a heart full of trust in God's guidance and protection. By lifting your eyes to Him, acknowledging your dependence on His mercy, and seeking His direction, you can navigate your journey with a sense of peace and assurance.

Applying the lessons from Psalms 123 to your life can help you approach your travels with confidence and faith. By seeking God's guidance, trusting in His provision, and recognizing your need for His mercy, you can embark on your journey with a heart ready to follow His lead and a spirit full of hope.

In conclusion, Psalms 123 is a powerful chapter to turn to when you leave to travel. The psalm's focus on looking to God for mercy and help, and its reflection on the challenges faced, reminds us of our dependence on God's guidance and protection. By reflecting on these verses and applying their lessons to your life, you can find confidence and reassurance in God's presence. Trusting in His provision, seeking His direction, and embracing His mercy can help you navigate your travels with faith and assurance. Through the timeless truths found in Psalms

123, you can draw strength and comfort from your faith, knowing that God is always with you and will never forsake you on your journey.

Conclusion

As we come to the end of this journey through the Bible, comparing it to our spiritual 911, we hope you have found comfort, guidance, and a deeper connection with God's Word. Each chapter has been carefully chosen to address the various situations we face in life, offering wisdom, conviction, and the assurance of God's presence and love. Just as we rely on emergency services in times of need, we can always turn to the Bible, knowing that God's Word is powerful, alive, and ready to provide exactly what we need when we need it.

Throughout this book, you have explored scriptures that offer help in times of worry, fear, opportunity, and more. You have seen how God's promises and teachings can transform your perspective, strengthen your faith, and guide your actions. The blessings learned from these scriptures are practical and applicable to everyday life, reminding us that God's Word is not just a historical document but a living, breathing guide for our spiritual journey.

As you move forward, we encourage you to continue making the Bible your first point of contact in all circumstances. Develop a habit of turning to scripture daily, not just in times of emergency, but as a regular practice of spiritual nourishment. Let the truths you've discovered in this book sink deep into your heart, guiding your thoughts, decisions, and actions.

Share the insights and blessings you have gained with others. Encourage your family, friends, and fellow believers to also turn to the Bible as their spiritual 911. Create a community that is rooted in God's Word, supporting each other with the wisdom and comfort found in scripture.

Remember, the journey with God's Word is lifelong. There will always be deeper understandings, and greater blessings as you continue to seek Him through the Bible. Keep a journal to record your reflections and the ways God speaks to you through His Word. Use it as a tool to see your spiritual growth and to remind yourself of God's faithfulness in every season.

In conclusion, let this book be a stepping stone to a richer, more profound relationship with God through His Word. Embrace the Bible as your ultimate guide, your source of wisdom, and your comfort in every situation. Trust in the promises of God, knowing that He is always with you, ready to provide for your needs and lead you on the path of righteousness. May your life be filled with the peace, joy, and assurance that come from a deep and abiding relationship with God through His Word.

Don't miss out!

Visit the website below and you can sign up to receive emails whenever Joshua Rhoades publishes a new book. There's no charge and no obligation.

https://books2read.com/r/B-A-AJLBB-UXBYE

BOOKS2READ

Connecting independent readers to independent writers.

Did you love *Spiritual 911- God's Word for Life's Emergency's*? Then you should read *Who Is on the Lord's Side? A Call to Righteousness*[1] by Joshua Rhoades!

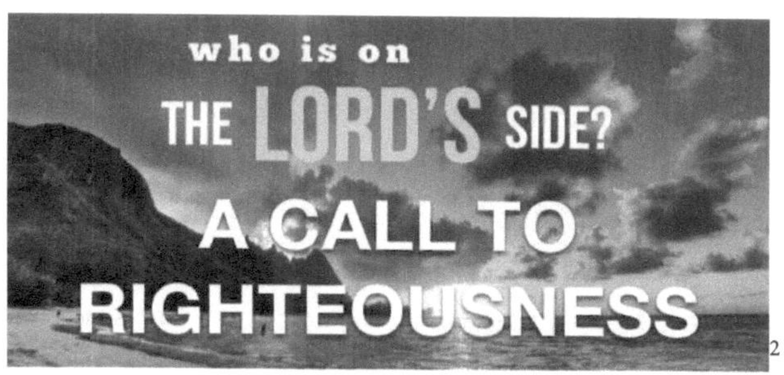

[2]

In a world increasingly marked by moral confusion and spiritual complacency, the question posed by Moses thousands of years ago, "Who is on the Lord's side?" resonates more urgently than ever. In an age where the lines between right and wrong are often blurred, and where societal pressures encourage compromise rather than conviction, there is a profound need for leaders who are willing to stand firm, lead with integrity, and call others to a life of righteousness. This book, "Who Is on the Lord's Side? A Call to Righteousness," seeks to provide a framework for understanding how to navigate the spiritual and moral challenges of our time, drawing from the timeless principles illustrated in the life of Moses.

The story of Moses standing at the gate of the camp and challenging the Israelites to declare their allegiance is more than just a historical account; it is a call to action that reverberates through the ages. Moses was faced with a rebellious and disobedient people, much like we encounter today in various forms. Yet, he did not shrink back from his responsibility. Instead, he stood firm, relying on his deep relationship with God to guide him in making difficult decisions that would restore

---

1. https://books2read.com/u/3J2wlA

2. https://books2read.com/u/3J2wlA

the people to righteousness. His leadership was not based on personal power or charisma, but on a profound commitment to justice, righteousness, and the authority of God.

This book explores the twelve principles drawn from Moses' leadership during this pivotal moment, principles that are as relevant now as they were in his time. These principles—such as bold leadership in crisis, unwavering commitment to God, the courage to stand alone, and a passion for God's glory—serve as a guide for anyone who seeks to lead others in a manner that honors God. Whether you are a pastor, a parent, a teacher, or simply someone striving to live out your faith in a challenging world, these principles will equip you to stand firm in your convictions and to inspire others to do the same.

"Who Is on the Lord's Side? A Call to Righteousness" is not just a manual for leadership; it is a call to every believer to examine their own life, to assess where they stand in their relationship with God, and to make the necessary changes to align their life with His will. In a time when the world desperately needs voices of truth and leaders of integrity, this book is a reminder that we are all called to be on the Lord's side, to stand for what is right, and to lead others into the light of God's righteousness.

As you read through the pages of this book, may you be challenged, inspired, and equipped to take your stand for the Lord. The journey of leading and standing firm in faith is not an easy one, but it is a journey worth taking. The question remains: Who is on the Lord's side? The time to answer is now.